Grade **8**

Prentice Hall
Math
Skill Builder

Unit 4: Geometry and Measurement

PEARSON
Prentice Hall

Boston, Massachusetts
Upper Saddle River, New Jersey

ISBN 0-13-201513-7

6 7 8 9 10 V016 14 13 12 11

TABLE OF CONTENTS

UNIT 4: Geometry and Measurement

SKILL 1 · ANGLES

A **ray** is a part of a line. It has one endpoint and extends without end in one direction. The diagram on the right shows $\overrightarrow{xy}$ (ray $\overrightarrow{xy}$). This ray has endpoint x and extends in the direction of y.

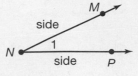

endoint

Two rays with a common endpoint form an **angle**.

The rays are the sides of the angle. The common endpoint is the **vertex**. You can use the angle symbol ($\angle$), the vertex, and a point on each side to name an angle. This angle could be named $\angle MNP$ or $\angle PNM$. You could also call this $\angle N$ or $\angle 1$.

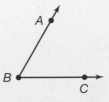

Example 1

Name the angle.

The vertex of the angle is B, so it will be the middle letter of the angle name. A point from each ray makes up the rest of the angle name, so the angle can be named $\angle ABC$, $\angle CBA$ or $\angle B$.

Example 2

Use a protractor to measure the angle.

Place the center mark of the protractor on the vertex and the 0° line on one side of the angle.

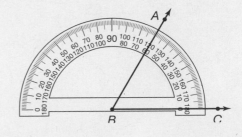

Beginning with 0°, follow the increasing degree numbers until you find the point where the other side of the angle meets the degree scale on the protractor. You may need to extend the sides of the angle to help you read the protractor.

The measure of $\angle ABC$ ($m\angle ABC$) is 60°.

GUIDED PRACTICE

Choose the best approximation of the measure of each angle.

Hint: Is the measure greater or less than 45°, 90°, 135°?

1.

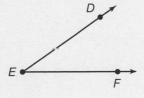

A 35°   **C** 60°
B 50°   **D** 95°

2.

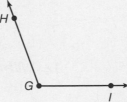

F 70°   **H** 105°
G 85°   **J** 140°

3.

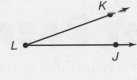

A 25°   **C** 45°
B 35°   **D** 55°

NOW YOU TRY IT!

Choose the best approximation of each angle.

1.

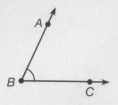

A	15°	C	90°
B	60°	D	125°

2.

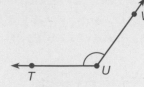

F	45°	H	90°
G	60°	J	125°

3.

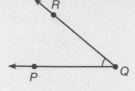

A	40°	C	80°
B	60°	D	90°

4.

F	65°	H	85°
G	75°	J	95°

5.

A	85°	C	125°
B	95°	D	135°

6.

F	15°	H	165°
G	135°	J	180°

7.

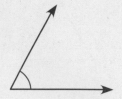

A	32°	C	82°
B	62°	D	112°

8.

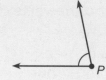

F	28°	H	78°
G	38°	J	98°

9.

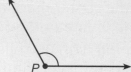

A	88°	C	118°
B	98°	D	138°

Problem Solving

10. When a beam of light strikes a flat mirror, the light reflects at the same angle at which it hits the mirror's surface. If light strikes a mirror at 63°, at what angle will the light reflect?

_____

TEST PREP

11. Classify point B in the figure.

A end point

B side

C vertex

D angle

12. What is the best approximation of the angle below?

F	75°	H	100°
G	90°	J	140°

SKILL 2 PARALLEL AND PERPENDICULAR LINES

A plane is an infinite flat surface. Lines in a plane that never meet are called **parallel** lines. Lines that intersect to form a right angle (90°) are called **perpendicular** lines. Lines that intersect two or more lines are called **transversals**.

A line segment is formed by two endpoints and all the points between them. A **midpoint** divides a line segment into two **congruent segments**. Congruent segments have equal lengths.

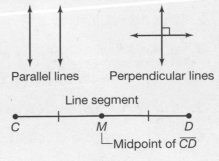

Parallel lines   Perpendicular lines

Line segment

Midpoint of $\overline{CD}$

Example 1

Write *parallel or perpendicular* to describe the lines formed by the left and right sides of a bulletin board.

Sketch a rectangle to represent a bulletin board. If the left and right sides were extended, they would never meet.

So, the lines formed are parallel.

Example 2

Use the figure to name a line segment, a midpoint, two congruent segments, and a transversal.

Two endpoints are S and U, so they form a line segment, $\overline{SU}$.

The midpoint of $\overline{SU}$ is M.

The midpoint divides a line segment into two congruent segments, so $\overline{MS}$ and $\overline{MU}$ are congruent.

Line $\overleftrightarrow{RU}$ intersects lines $\overleftrightarrow{RS}$ and $\overleftrightarrow{TU}$, so $\overleftrightarrow{RU}$ is a transversal.

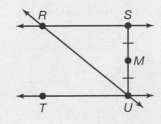

GUIDED PRACTICE

1. Write *parallel or perpendicular* to describe the lines formed by this book.

   a. Top and bottom sides _____

   b. Top and left sides _____

2. Use the figure to name each of the following.

   a. A line segment _____

   b. A midpoint _____

   c. Two congruent segments _____

   d. A transversal _____

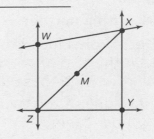

NOW YOU TRY IT!

Write the word that describes the lines or line segments.

1. the strings on a guitar _____

2. the marks left by a skidding car _____

3. sidewalks on opposite sides of a street _____

4. the segments that make up a + sign _____

5. the wires suspended between telephone poles _____

6. the hands of a clock at 9:00 P.M. _____

7. two palm trees in Los Angeles _____

Use the figure to name each pair of angles or lines.

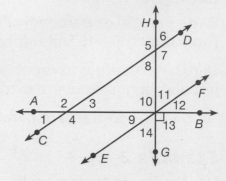

8. a pair of parallel lines _____

9. a pair of perpendicular lines _____

10. a pair of corresponding angles _____

11. a pair of alternate interior angles _____

12. a pair of vertical angles _____

13. three angles that are congruent

    to ∠6 _____

14. Use a ruler to draw a segment bisector of $\overline{UV}$.

15. Use a ruler and a rectangular object to draw a perpendicular bisector of $\overline{XY}$.

A LITTLE SOMETHING DIFFERENT...

Work with a partner.

a. Decide on a location in the classroom that the two of you will try to get to by following these directions.

b. Have one of the two of you roll a number cube.

c. If you roll an even number take three steps parallel to your destination. If you roll an odd number then take three steps perpendicular.

d. Continue to roll the cube until you and your partner reach your goal.

MISSING ANGLES

Use facts about angles and lines to find the measurements of missing angles. **Supplementary angles** are two angles with measures that have a sum of 180°. **Complementary angles** are two angles with measures that have a sum of 90°.

The diagram to the right is made up of several types of angles.

The **interior angles** are the four angles between the two lines. The **exterior angles** are the four angles outside the two lines.

Corresponding angles are on the same side of the transveral and are congruent when the transveral crosses parallel lines.

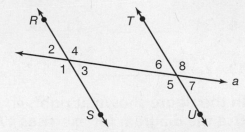

$\overline{RS}$ is parallel to $\overline{TU}$.

Example 1

Find the measure of the complement and the suplement to ∠ABC.

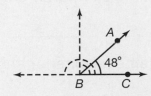

Subtract from 90° to find the measure of the complementary angle.

$$90° - 48° = 42°$$

The complement of ∠ABC measures 42°.

Subtract from 180° to find the measure of the supplementary angle.

$$180° - 48° = 132°$$

The supplement of ∠ABC measures 132°.

Example 2

In the diagram, $\overleftrightarrow{JK}$ and $\overleftrightarrow{LM}$ are parallel. If ∠1 = 103°, find the measure of the other angles.

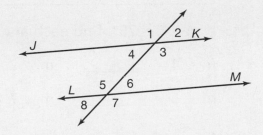

∠2, ∠4, ∠6, ∠8 = 77°

∠3, ∠5, ∠7 = 103°.

GUIDED PRACTICE

Find each angle measure.

1. Complement of 33° _____

2. Complement of 87° _____

3. Supplement of 95° _____

4. Supplement of 121° _____

Refer to the transversal diagram above and find the measure of each angle if 1 = 116°.

5. ∠2 = _____   6. ∠3 = _____   7. ∠4 = _____   8. ∠5 = _____

NOW YOU TRY IT!

Find the measure of the complement of each angle measure.

1. 82° _____   2. 31° _____   3. 7° _____   4. 64° _____

5. 35° _____   6. 0.7° _____   7. 50° _____   8. 12° _____

Find the measure of the supplement of each angle measure.

9. 34° _____   10. 100° _____   11. 67° _____   12. 125° _____

13. 2.3° _____   14. 53° _____   15. 176° _____   16. 84° _____

In the figure shown at right, $\overleftrightarrow{PQ}$ is parallel to $\overleftrightarrow{RS}$. Use the diagram for exercises 17–21.

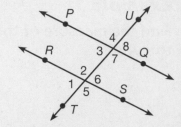

17. Name all interior angles.

   _____

18. Name all exterior angles.

   _____

19. Name the transversal.

   _____

20. Name four pairs of corresponding angles.

   _____

21. If m ∠6 = 75°, find each angle measure.

   m ∠1 = _____   m ∠2 = _____   m ∠3 = _____   m ∠4 = _____

   m ∠5 = _____   m ∠7 = _____   m ∠8 = _____

Problem Solving

22. Light strikes a flat mirror at an angle of 63° and is reflected at the same angle. What is the measure of the angle between the angle at which light strikes the mirror and the angle at which it is reflected? (Hint: The three angles add to form a straight angle.)   _____

TEST PREP

23. What is the complement to 19°?

   A 19°   **C** 171°

   B 71°   **D** 251°

24. How is an angle measuring 63° best classified?

   F right angle   **H** obtuse angle

   G acute angle   **J** straight angle

SKILL 4 TRIANGLES AND QUADRILATERALS

Triangles are three-sided figures. You can classify triangles by the number of congruent sides they have.

Equilateral
3 congruent sides

Isosceles
2 congruent sides

Scalene
No congruent sides

Another way to classify triangles is by their angles.

acute triangle
three acute angles

right triangle
one right angle

obtuse triangle
one obtuse angle

Quadrilaterals are four-sided figures.
Quadrilaterals can be classified by their properties.

	Parallelogram	Two pairs of parallel sides; two pairs of congruent sides
	Rectangle	Parallelogram with four right angles
	Square	Rectangle with four congruent sides
	Rhombus	Parallelogram with four congruent sides
	Trapezoid	Only one pair of parallel sides

Example 1

Classify the triangle by its sides and its angles.

No two sides of the triangle are congruent, so triangle *ABC* is scalene. The triangle has a right angle. Triangle *ABC* is also a right triangle.

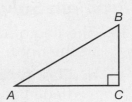

Example 2

Classify this quadrilateral in as many ways as you can.

The quadrilateral has two pairs of parallel sides, four congruent sides, and no right angles.

The quadrilateral is a rhombus and a parallelogram.

GUIDED PRACTICE

Classify each figure in as many ways as you can.

1. _____

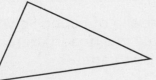

2. _____

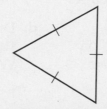

3. _____

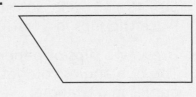

NOW YOU TRY IT!

Classify each triangle by its sides and by its angles.

1. _____
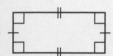

2. _____
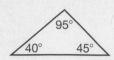

3. _____

Classify each quadrilateral in as many ways as you can.

4. _____
_____
_____

5. _____
_____
_____

6. _____
_____
_____

Find the missing angle in each triangle or quadrilateral.

7. *x* = _____

8. *n* = _____
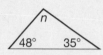

9. *u* = _____

Problem Solving

10. The flag of the Republic of the Congo is shown at the right.

   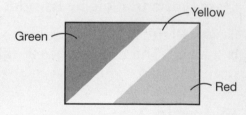

   a. Classify the red and green portions of the flag in as many ways as you can. (Hint: The top edge of the green region is slightly longer than the height of the flag.)

   _____

   b. Classify the yellow portion of the flag in as many ways as you can. _____

A LITTLE SOMETHING DIFFERENT...

a. Write the angles 75°, 70°, 65°, 60°, 55°, 50°, 45°, 40°, 35°, 30° on slips of paper. Place the slips in a hat.

b. Draw two slips of paper from the hat. The two angles you get will be two angles in a triangle.

c. Solve for the third angle. What is the missing angle? _____

d. Draw one more slip of paper. Solve for the fourth angle in a quadrilateral. What is the missing angle?

_____

POLYGONS

A **polygon** is a geometric figure with at least three sides. A polygon is classified by the number of sides it has. In a **regular** polygon, all of the sides and all of the angles are congruent.

3 sides
triangle

4 sides
quadrilateral

5 sides
pentagon

6 sides
hexagon

8 sides
octagon

You can find the sum of the measures of the angles of a polygon by dividing it into triangles.

Example 1

Name the polygon and determine if it is regular.

Count the sides.
There are six sides, so the polygon is a hexagon.

Are the sides and angles congruent?
Yes, so the hexagon is regular.

The polygon is a regular hexagon.

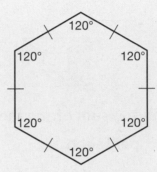

Example 2

Find the sum of the measures of a 5-sided polygon, called a pentagon.

Choose a vertex and divide the figure into triangles.
There are three triangles.

Multiply the number of triangles by 180°: 3 × 180 = 540.

The sum of the measures of the angles of a pentagon is 540°.

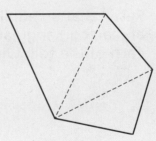

GUIDED PRACTICE

Name each polygon and determine if it is regular.

a. _____   b. _____

Find the sum of the measures of the angles of each polygon.

a. _____   b. _____   c. _____   d. _____

NOW YOU TRY IT!

Tell why each polygon is not a regular polygon.

1. _____

_____

2. _____

_____

3. _____

_____

In each design, identify as many polygons as you can.

4. _____

_____

5. _____

_____

6. _____

_____

Find the sum of the measures of the angles of each polygon.

7. pentagon

_____

8. 10-sided polygon

_____

9. 32-sided polygon

_____

10. Recall that an equilateral polygon has all sides congruent, and an equiangular polygon has all angles congruent. Draw each of the following, if possible.

c. equiangular triangle that is not equilateral

_____

a. equiangular hexagon that is not regular

_____

b. equilateral quadrilateral that is not regular

_____

TEST PREP

11. How many polygons does this face have?

A 0   C 4
B 2   D 5

12. Which of the following is a parallelogram with four congruent sides?

F trapezoid   H rhombus
G rectangle   J pentagon

TEST PREP

Circle each correct answer.

Use the figure below to answer questions 1–2.

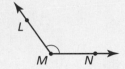

1. What is the vertex of the angle?

A L   **C** M

B N   **D** MN

2. Estimate the measure of angle LMN.

F 15°   **H** 65°

G 35°   **J** 110°

Use the figure below to answer questions 3–4.

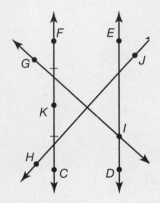

3. Which pair of lines in the figure is perpendicular to each other?

A $\overleftrightarrow{CK}$ and $\overleftrightarrow{KF}$

B $\overleftrightarrow{GI}$ and $\overleftrightarrow{HJ}$

C $\overleftrightarrow{HJ}$ and $\overleftrightarrow{ED}$

D $\overleftrightarrow{FC}$ and $\overleftrightarrow{ED}$

4. Which pair of lines is parallel to each other?

F $\overleftrightarrow{CK}$ and $\overleftrightarrow{KF}$

G $\overleftrightarrow{GI}$ and $\overleftrightarrow{HJ}$

H $\overleftrightarrow{HJ}$ and $\overleftrightarrow{ED}$

J $\overleftrightarrow{FC}$ and $\overleftrightarrow{ED}$

5. Classify the triangle by its sides.

A Scalene

B Right

C Isosceles

D Equilateral

6. Which is always true of a regular polygon?

F it has exactly four sides

G all angles are unequal

H all sides are congruent

J the sum of the internal angles = 360°

7. What is the sum of the angles of a octagon?

A 180°   **C** 720°

B 360°   **D** 1,080°

8. Which is an element of a trapezoid?

F 2 pairs of parallel sides

G 4 right angles

H 1 pair of parallel sides

J 4 congruent sides

Use the figure to answer questions 9–10.

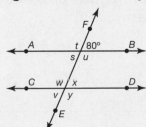

9. Find the value of the *t*.

A 10°   **C** 110°

B 80°   **D** 170°

10. Find the value of the *v*.

F 10°   **H** 90°

G 80°   **J** 180°

You have learned that the interior angles of a triangle measure 180°. Now prove it!

1. Trace and cut a triangle out of paper and label each angle A, B, C.

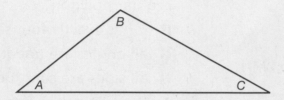

2. Next, cut your triangle into three pieces so that each piece has one of the labeled angles.

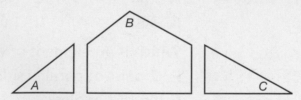

3. Rearrange the labeled angles so that they align in a straight line. Explain how this proves that the interior angles of a triangle measure 180°.

_____

_____

_____

4. Try the same activity with a different triangle. Do you get the same results?   _____

SKILL 6 PERIMETER

The distance around the outside of a figure is known as the **perimeter**. To find the perimeter of a given geometric figure, you add the lengths of the sides.

Example

Find the length of the unknown side. Then find the perimeter.

In a rectangle, opposite sides are equal, so the height of the right side is equal to the height of the left side. The left side is 5 ft, so the two segments on the right side also equal 5 ft. One segment is 3 ft, so, the other is 5 − 3, or 2 ft.
$8 + 2 + 2 + 3 + 10 + 5 = 30$
The perimeter is *30 feet*.

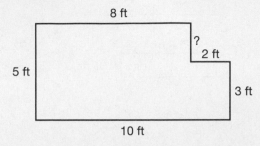

GUIDED PRACTICE

Find each perimeter by adding the lengths of the sides.

1.

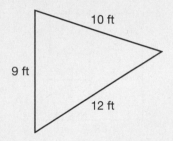

_____

2.

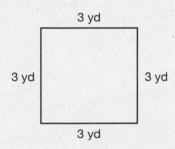

_____

Find the length of the unknown side.

3.

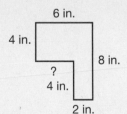

a. In a rectangle, opposite sides are _____.

b. $6 -$ _____ $=$ _____

c. The unknown side is _____.

4.

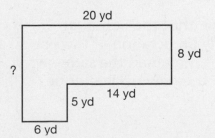

5.

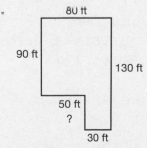

_____   _____

NOW YOU TRY IT!

Find the perimeter.

1.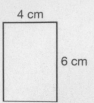
4 cm
6 cm

_____

2.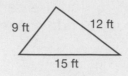
9 ft 12 ft
15 ft

_____

3.
3 m
3 m

_____

4.
1.4 mi
0.35 mi

_____

5.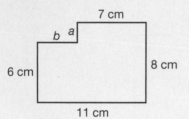
4 in.
4 in.
2 in.
5 in.

_____

6.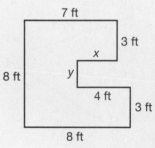
11 km
8 km
3 km 3 km

_____

Find the length of each unknown side.

7.
7 cm
b a
6 cm 8 cm
11 cm

8.
12 in.
12 in.
c 16 in.
4 in.
d

9.
7 ft
3 ft
x
8 ft y
4 ft
3 ft
8 ft

a = _____   b = _____   c = _____   d = _____   x = _____   y = _____

Problem Solving

10. The triangular base of a skyscraper has a perimeter of 89 m. If two of the sides have lengths 30 m and 35 m, what is the length of the third side? _____

 LITTLE SOMETHING DIFFERENT...

The Pentagon in Arlington, Virginia is the home of the U.S. Department of Defense. The Pentagon is one of the world's largest office building.

The length of one of the outer walls of the building is 921 ft.

a. Find the perimeter of the pentagon's outer wall. _____

b. Imagine that the Pentagon was actually an octagon. If the side lengths remained the same, what would the new perimeter be?

_____

SKILL 7 AREA OF RECTANGLES AND SQUARES

The **area** of a figure is the amount of surface it covers. Area is usually measured by the number of unit squares of the same size that fit into the figure. If a figure is labeled with inches, then the area is expressed in **square inches (in²)**. A square inch is a square whose sides measure one inch. A **square centimeter (cm²)** is a square whose sides measure one centimeter.

The **width** of a rectangle is the distance of the shorter side. The **length** is the distance of the longer side. The area of any rectangle is equal to the length times the width. The area of a square is the length of the side multiplied by itself.

Example

Find the area of the rectangle.

Each side is measured in centimeters, so the area will be measured in square centimeters (cm²). Find the area by multiplying length and width. 8 cm × 5 cm = 40 cm²

The area of the rectangle is 40 square centimeters.

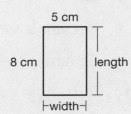

GUIDED PRACTICE

Find the area of each rectangle.

1.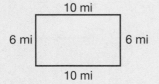

   a. What is the width? _____

   b. What is the length? _____

   c. Multiply width and length to find the area. _____

2. 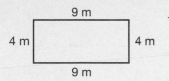   _____

3. 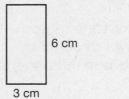   _____

4. 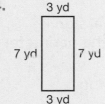   _____

5. 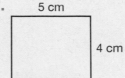   _____

6. 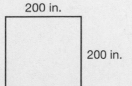   _____

7.   _____

NOW YOU TRY IT!

Find the missing measurement for each rectangle.

1. Area = _____

   Width = 7 ft

   Length = 9 ft

2. Area = 24 cm^2

   Width = _____

   Length = 6 cm

3. Area = 84 in^2

   Width = 7 in.

   Length = _____

4. Area = 11.5 m^2

   Width = 5 m

   Length = _____

5. Area = _____

   Width = 5.875 in.

   Length = 4 in.

6. Area = 12.46 cm^2

   Width = _____

   Length = 7 cm

Find the area of each figure.

7. Square with sides of length 8 ft _____

8. Rectangle with sides 4.7 m and 7.3 m _____

9. Square with sides of length 21 cm _____

10. Rectangle with sides 8.3 m and 5.2 m _____

11. Rectangle with sides 9 in. and 4 in. _____

Problem Solving

12. Shelly plans to paint a wall in her bedroom. The wall is 11 ft long and 8 ft high. She needs enough paint to cover how much area? _____

13. The Food Bank for Monterey County (California) set a record by baking a lasagne with an area of 490 ft^2. If the lasagne was 70 ft long, how wide was it? _____

14. Santiago is building a square whirlpool. If the area will be 49 ft^2, how long will one side be? _____

TEST PREP

15. A map of the Yellowstone region showed it has an area of 60 mi by 60 mi. How many square miles were shown on the map?

    A 120 mi^2 **C** 360 mi^2

    B 240 mi^2 **D** 3,600 mi^2

16. Each side of a hexagonal sign is 8 inches long. What is the perimeter of the sign?

    F 16 in.   **H** 64 in.

    G 48 in.   **J** 80 in.

 # SQUARES AND SQUARE ROOTS

You know that $9 \times 9 = 81$. The factors, 9×9, can also be written as 9^2, or 9 *squared*.

A **perfect square** is the square of a whole number. The number 81, is a perfect square because it is the square of 9.

You can also say that 9 is the **square root** of 81. The square root of a number is the length of the side of a square with an area equal to the number.

The area of the square at the right is 81 square units. The length of a side is the square root of 81, or 9 units.

81

9

Use a **radical sign**, $\sqrt{}$, to write a square root: $\sqrt{81} = 9$.

Example 1

Determine if 64 and 75 are perfect squares.

What number times itself equals 64?
$8 \times 8 = 64$
So, 64 is a perfect square.

What number times itself equals 75?
$8 \times 8 = 64$, $9 \times 9 = 81$. No whole number times itself equals 75.
So, 75 is *not* a perfect square.

Example 2

Find the square root of 16.

Think: What number times itself equals 16?
$\qquad 4 \times 4 = 4^2 = 16$
$\qquad$ So, $\sqrt{16} = 4$.

GUIDED PRACTICE

Determine if each number is a perfect square.

1. 24 _____   **2.** 36 _____   **3.** 49 _____   **4.** 121 _____

Find each square root.

5. 9 = _____ × _____   Therefore $\sqrt{9}$ = _____

6. 25 = _____ × _____   Therefore $\sqrt{25}$ = _____

7. 4 = _____ × _____   Therefore $\sqrt{4}$ = _____

8. 100 = _____ × _____   Therefore $\sqrt{100}$ = _____

9. 400 = _____ × _____   Therefore $\sqrt{400}$ = _____

10. 2500 = _____ × _____   Therefore $\sqrt{2500}$ = _____

NOW YOU TRY IT!

Determine if each number is a perfect square.

1. 90 _____
2. 225 _____
3. 49 _____
4. 28 _____

5. 289 _____
6. 144 _____
7. 240 _____
8. 1000 _____

Find each square root.

9. $\sqrt{196}$ _____
10. $\sqrt{4}$ _____
11. $\sqrt{289}$ _____
12. $\sqrt{16}$ _____

13. $\sqrt{361}$ _____
14. $\sqrt{64}$ _____
15. $\sqrt{1}$ _____
16. $\sqrt{25}$ _____

17. $\sqrt{9}$ _____
18. $\sqrt{484}$ _____
19. $\sqrt{256}$ _____
20. $\sqrt{400}$ _____

Use a calculator to find each square root. Round the answer to two decimal places.

21. $\sqrt{10}$ _____
22. $\sqrt{48}$ _____
23. $\sqrt{28}$ _____
24. $\sqrt{55}$ _____

25. $\sqrt{72}$ _____
26. $\sqrt{37}$ _____
27. $\sqrt{86}$ _____
28. $\sqrt{98}$ _____

29. $\sqrt{946}$ _____
30. $\sqrt{14}$ _____
31. $\sqrt{62}$ _____
32. $\sqrt{316}$ _____

33. $\sqrt{68}$ _____
34. $\sqrt{146}$ _____
35. $\sqrt{76}$ _____
36. $\sqrt{521}$ _____

37. $\sqrt{813}$ _____
38. $\sqrt{83}$ _____
39. $\sqrt{23}$ _____
40. $\sqrt{617}$ _____

41. $\sqrt{35}$ _____
42. $\sqrt{123}$ _____
43. $\sqrt{51}$ _____
44. $\sqrt{463}$ _____

45. $\sqrt{583}$ _____
46. $\sqrt{96}$ _____
47. $\sqrt{203}$ _____
48. $\sqrt{1200}$ _____

Problem Solving

49. The largest pyramid in Egypt, built almost 5,000 years ago, covers an area of about 63,300 yd^2. Find the length of each side of the square base. _____

A LITTLE SOMETHING DIFFERENT...

Put the expressions in order from least to greatest. Then use the correct letters to answer the question.

It lives without a body, hears without ears, speaks without a mouth and is born in the air. What is it?

An _____ _____ _____ _____
       a.   b.   c.   d.

a. $-\sqrt{36}$ E. -6 F. 6

b. $-\sqrt{9}$ C. -3 D. 3

c. $\sqrt{4}$ H. 2   I. 16

d. $\sqrt{25}$ O. 5   P. 7

THE PYTHAGOREAN THEOREM

SKILL 9

The **hypotenuse** of a right triangle is the side opposite the right angle and is the longest side. The other two sides are called **legs**. In the triangle at the right, sides a and b are the legs. Side c is the hypotenuse.

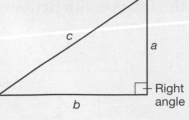

The **Pythagorean Theorem** states that the sum of the squares of the lengths of the legs of a right triangle is equal to the square of the length of the hypotenuse.

This can be written algebraically as $a^2 + b^2 = c^2$.

Example 1

Name the hypotenuse and legs of the right triangle.

Side h is opposite the right angle, so it is the hypotenuse.

Sides i and j are the legs.

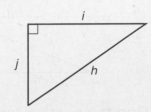

Example 2

Find the missing length.

Use the Pythagorean Theorem to find the length of side c.

Substitute 9 for a and 12 for b.

Square 9 and 12.

Add.

Find $\sqrt{225}$

$a^2 + b^2 = c^2$

$9^2 + 12^2 = c^2$

$81 + 144 = c^2$

$225 = c^2$

$15 = c$

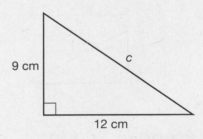

The length of the hypotenuse is 15 cm.

GUIDED PRACTICE

1. **Name the hypotenuse and legs of each triangle.**

a.

Hypotenuse _____

Legs   _____

b.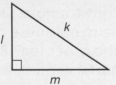

Hypotenuse _____

Legs   _____

c.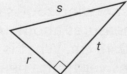

Hypotenuse _____

Legs   _____

2. **Find the missing length in each right triangle.**

a.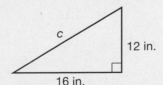

_____

b.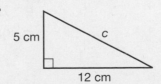

_____

c.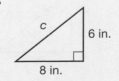

_____

NOW YOU TRY IT!

Use the Pythagorean Theorem to write an equation expressing the relationship between the legs and the hypotenuse for each triangle.

1. _____

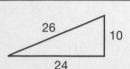

2. _____

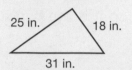

3. _____

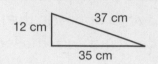

Determine if each triangle is a right triangle.

4. _____

5. _____

6. _____

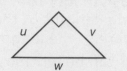

Find the missing length in each right triangle.

7. $t =$ _____

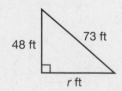

8. $d =$ _____

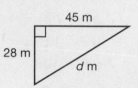

9. $m =$ _____

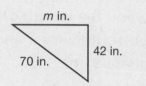

Problem Solving

10. The state of Colorado is shaped like a rectangle, with a base measuring about 385 mi and a height of about 275 mi. About how far is it from the northwest corner to the southeast corner of Colorado?

_____

11. A drawing tool is shaped like a right triangle. One leg measures about 14.48 cm, and the hypotenuse measures 20.48 cm. What is the length of the other leg? Round your answer to the nearest hundredth of a centimeter.

_____

TEST PREP

12. Find the missing length.

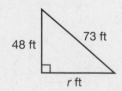

48 ft   73 ft   r ft

A 5   **C** 55
B 25   **D** 121

13. Which of the following is a perfect square?

F 72   **H** 144
G 90   **J** 156

SKILL 10 TRIGONOMETRY

The side opposite the right angle in a right triangle is the **hypotenuse**. Think of each of the other two sides, or legs, as being *adjacent* to one of the acute angles and *opposite* the other acute angle.

In △ABC, the hypotenuse is $\overline{AC}$.

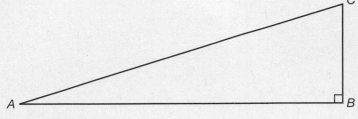

Side $\overline{AB}$ is the **adjacent leg** to ∠A.

Side $\overline{AB}$ is the **opposite leg** to ∠C.

Side $\overline{BC}$ is the **adjacent leg** to ∠C.

Side $\overline{BC}$ is the **opposite leg** to ∠A.

For any right triangle, the lengths of the hypotenuse, an adjacent leg, and an opposite leg may be compared by using three common **trigonometric ratios**.

Sine

The sine of x is

$\sin(x) = \dfrac{\text{opposite}}{\text{hypotenuse}}$

Cosine

The cosine of x is

$\cos(x) = \dfrac{\text{adjacent}}{\text{hypotenuse}}$

Tangent

The tangent of x is

$\tan(x) = \dfrac{\text{opposite}}{\text{adjacent}}$

Example

Evaluate the trigonometric ratios for ∠EDF in the triangle at the right to the nearest hundredth.

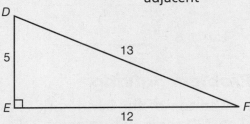

Identify the sides: The hypotenuse is $\overline{DF}$. The opposite leg is $\overline{EF}$. The adjacent leg is $\overline{DE}$.

Find the trigonometric ratios:

$\sin ∠EDF = \dfrac{\text{opposite}}{\text{hypotenuse}} = \dfrac{12}{13} = 0.92$

$\cos ∠EDF = \dfrac{\text{adjacent}}{\text{hypotenuse}} = \dfrac{5}{13} = 0.38$

$\tan ∠EDF = \dfrac{\text{opposite}}{\text{adjacent}} = \dfrac{12}{5} = 2.4$

GUIDED PRACTICE

1. **Evaluate the trigonometric ratios for ∠HFG in the triangle at the right to the nearest hundredth.**

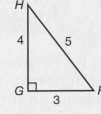

   a. Name the hypotenuse. _____

   b. Name the opposite leg to ∠HFG. _____

   c. Name the adjacent leg to ∠HFG. _____   **d.** $\sin ∠HFG = \dfrac{\qquad}{\text{hypotenuse}} = $ _____

   e. $\cos ∠HFG = \dfrac{\qquad}{\text{hypotenuse}} = $ _____   **f.** $\tan ∠HFG = \dfrac{\qquad}{\text{adjacent}} = $ _____

2. **Evaluate the trigonometric ratios for ∠XYZ in the triangle at the right to the nearest hundredth.**

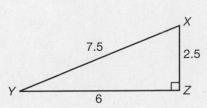

   a. Hypotenuse _____   **b.** Opposite leg _____

   c. Adjacent leg _____   **d.** $\cos ∠XYZ = $ _____

   e. $\sin ∠XYZ = $ _____   **f.** $\tan ∠XYZ = $ _____

NOW YOU TRY IT!

Use the lengths of the sides to evaluate the sine, cosine, and tangent ratios for each of the labeled angles. Round to the nearest hundredth.

1. sin ∠A = _____

cos ∠A = _____

tan ∠A = _____

12 ft   15 ft   9 ft   A

2. sin ∠B = _____

cos ∠B = _____

tan ∠B = _____

$6\frac{1}{2}$ in.   B $2\frac{1}{2}$ in.   6 in.

3. sin ∠C = _____

cos ∠C = _____

tan ∠C = _____

18 m   18 m   C

4. sin ∠D = _____

cos ∠D = _____

tan ∠D = _____

2.8 cm   D   4.5 cm   5.3 cm

5. sin ∠E = _____

cos ∠E = _____

tan ∠E = _____

E   77 in.   36 in.

6. sin ∠F = _____

cos ∠F = _____

tan ∠F = _____

4   3   F

Problem Solving

7. The top of the Landmark Tower in Yokohama, Japan, forms a 72° angle with a point $315\frac{1}{2}$ ft away from the tower's base, as shown. Given that tan ∠C ≈ 3.077 how tall is the Landmark Tower?

_____

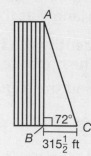

A   72°   C   B $315\frac{1}{2}$ ft

A LITTLE SOMETHING DIFFERENT...

In the map below, Albion St. and Arlington St. are perpendicular to each other. The streets and landmarks create two right triangles.

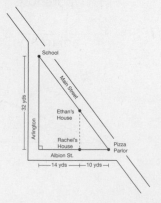

School   Main Street   Ethan's House   32 yds   Arlington   Rachel's House   Pizza Parlor   Albion St.   14 yds   10 yds

a. What is the distance down Main Street between school and the pizza parlor?

_____

b. If Ethan's house is 7 yards down Main Street from the school, what is the distance down Main Street between Ethan's house and the pizza parlor?

_____

What is the shortest distance between Rachel's house and Ethan's house?

_____

 AREA OF TRIANGLES

The area of a triangle equals half the area of a rectangle that has the same base and height as the triangle. You can find the area of a triangle by calculating the area of the rectangle that surrounds it and dividing that in half. You can also use the area formula for a triangle.

Example

Find the area of this triangle.

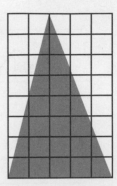

Method One: The area of the rectangular grid is 5 × 8, or 40 square units. Since the triangle on the grid covers only half of the squares, the area of the triangle is half of 40, or 20 square units.

Method Two: Use the formula $\frac{1}{2}$(**base × height**) = **area**.

The base of the triangle is 5 units.

The height of the triangle is 8 units. 5 × 8 ÷ 2 = 20

The area of the triangle is **20 square units**.

GUIDED PRACTICE

Find each area.

1.

Base _____ Height _____

$\frac{1}{2}$(_____ × _____) = _____

Area _____

2.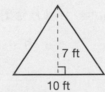

10 ft

Base _____ Height _____

$\frac{1}{2}$(_____ × _____) = _____

Area _____

3.
6 m
3 m
_____

4.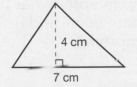
4 cm
7 cm
_____

5.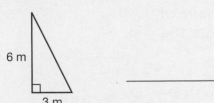
10 ft
12 ft
_____

6.
8 cm
4 cm
_____

NOW YOU TRY IT!

Find the area of each triangle. The dashed line is a height.

1.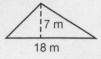
7 m
18 m

_____

2.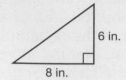
6 in.
8 in.

_____

3.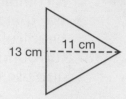
13 cm   11 cm

_____

4.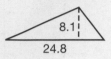
8.1
24.8

_____

5.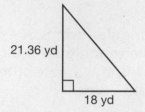
21.36 yd
18 yd

_____

6.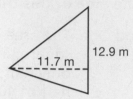
12.9 m
11.7 m

_____

7.
8.3 ft
7 ft

_____

8.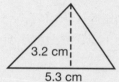
3.2 cm
5.3 cm

_____

9.
7.8 mi
4.7 mi

_____

Find the area if *b* is the base and *h* is the height of the triangle.

10. $b = 12$ ft, $h = 5$ ft

_____

11. $h = 9$ cm, $b = 11$ cm

_____

12. $b = 4.2$ mi, $h = 6$ mi

_____

13. $h = 7.3$, $b = 12.4$

_____

14. $b = 8.37$ in., $h = 10.4$ in.

_____

15. $h = 2.8$ km, $b = 5.8$ km

_____

Problem Solving

16. The state of New Hampshire has the approximate shape of a triangle with base 90 mi and height 180 mi. Estimate the area of New Hampshire.

_____

TEST PREP

17. What is the area of the triangle?

   A 6.1 ft^2

   B 4.37 ft^2

   C 7.34 ft^2

   D 8.74 ft^2

4 ft
2.185 ft

18. The leg adjacent to $\angle CAB$ is 6 ft long. Sin $\angle CAB$ equals 0.8. What is the length of the hypotenuse?

   F 6 ft.   **H** 10 ft.

   G 8 ft.   **J** 12 ft.

 # AREA OF PARALLELOGRAMS AND TRAPEZOIDS

The *height* of a parallelogram or trapezoid is the length of a perpendicular segment that connects two parallel bases. The formula to find the area of a parallelogram is $A = bh$ where A is area, b is the base, and h is height.

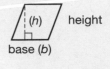

The formula to find the area of a trapezoid is $A = \frac{1}{2}h(b_1 + b_2)$ where A is area, b_1 is one base, and b_2 is the other base.

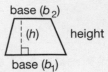

Example 1

Find the area of the parallelogram.

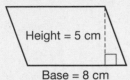

$A = bh$ — Use the formula for area of a parallelogram.

$\quad = 8 \cdot 5$ — Substitute 8 for b and 5 for h.

$\quad = 40$ — Multiply.

The area is 40 cm^2.

Example 2

Find the area of the trapezoid.

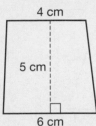

$A = \frac{1}{2}h(b_1 + b_2)$ — Use the formula for area of a trapezoid.

$\quad = \frac{1}{2} \cdot 5(6 + 4)$ — Substitute 5 for h, 6 for b_1, and 4 for b_2.

$\quad = \frac{1}{2} \cdot 5(10)$ — Add.

$\quad = 25$ — Multiply.

The area is 25 cm^2.

GUIDED PRACTICE

Find the area of each parallelogram or trapezoid.

1. Base _____

   Height _____

   Area _____

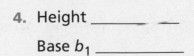
12 in.

9 in.

2. Base _____

   Height _____

   Area _____

8 in.

10 in.

6 in.

3. Height _____

   Base b_1 _____

   Base b_2 _____

   $b_1 + b_2$ _____

   Area _____

15 cm

9 cm

4. Height _____

   Base b_1 _____

   Base b_2 _____

   $b_1 + b_2$ _____

   Area _____

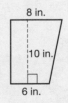
50 cm

30 cm

20 cm

NOW YOU TRY IT!

Find the area of each parallelogram.

1.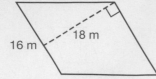

2.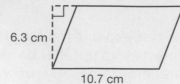

3.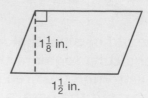

_____   _____   _____

Find the area of each trapezoid.

4.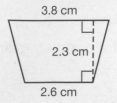

5.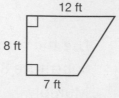

6.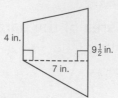

_____   _____   _____

Problem Solving

7. A section of a sidewalk is shown at the right. It is shaped like a parallelogram. The measurements are shown. Find the area. _____

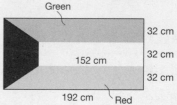

8. The flag of Kuwait is shown at the right. Find each area.

   a. Black region _____

   b. Green region (top stripe) _____

   c. White region _____

   d. Red region (bottom stripe) _____

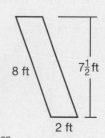

A LITTLE SOMETHING DIFFERENT...

Use the letters that correspond with the correct answer to solve the riddle.

I have eyes but cannot see. What am I?

   ___ ___ ___ ___ ___ ___
   1   2   3   4   5   6

Parallelogram

1. base = 5; height = 6; Area = ?
     C 11   **P** 30

2. base = 9; height = ?; Area = 81
     O 9   **H** 18

3. base = 5; height = 7; Area = ?
     T 35   **O** 245

Trapezoid

4. b1 = 7; b2 = 8; height = 5; Area = ?
     A 37.5   **T** 75

5. b1 = 3; b2 = 5; height = 7; Area = ?
     L 105   **T** 28

6. b1 = 8.4; b2 = 4.9; height = 5.1; Area = ?
     A 18.4   **O** 33.91

AREA OF COMPOUND SHAPES

Not all geometric figures are shapes with which you are familiar. Some of them, however, can be divided into familiar shapes.

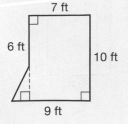

Example

Find the area of the figure.

This shape can be divided into a triangle and a rectangle.

Find the height of the triangle. Subtract the length of the known portion from the length of the opposite side: $10 - 6 = 4$.

Find the base of the triangle. Subtract the side of the rectangle from the base of the figure: $9 - 7 = 2$.

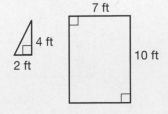

$$\text{Area of a triangle} = \tfrac{1}{2}(b \times h) \qquad \text{Area of a rectangle} = b \times h$$
$$= \tfrac{1}{2}(2 \times 4) \qquad\qquad\qquad\quad = 7 \times 10$$
$$= \tfrac{1}{2}(8) \qquad\qquad\qquad\qquad = 70 \text{ ft}^2$$
$$= 4 \text{ ft}^2$$

Total area = area of triangle + area of rectangle
$$= 4 + 70$$
$$= 74$$

The total area is 74 ft^2.

GUIDED PRACTICE

Find the area of the figure shown.

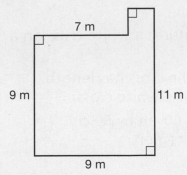

1. Divide the figure into two squares.

2. Find the length of a side of the large square. _____

3. Find the length of a side of the small square. _____

4. Find the area of the large square. _____

5. Find the area of the small square. _____

6. Find the total area. _____ + _____ = _____

NOW YOU TRY IT!

Find the area of each figure.

1.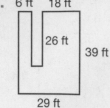
6 ft 18 ft
26 ft
39 ft
29 ft

2.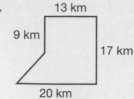
13 km
9 km
17 km
20 km

3.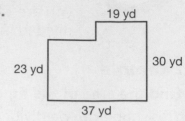
19 yd
23 yd
30 yd
37 yd

_____

4.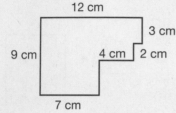
12 cm
3 cm
9 cm 4 cm 2 cm
7 cm

5.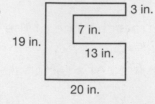
3 in.
7 in.
19 in.
13 in.
20 in.

6.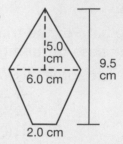
5.0 cm
6.0 cm
9.5 cm
2.0 cm

_____

7.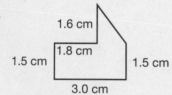
1.6 cm
1.8 cm
1.5 cm   1.5 cm
3.0 cm

8.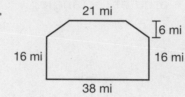
21 mi
6 mi
16 mi   16 mi
38 mi

9.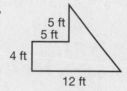
5 ft
5 ft
4 ft
12 ft

_____

Problem Solving

10. The flag of Switzerland features a white cross on a red background.

   a. Each of the 12 sides of the cross has length 15 cm. Find the area of the white cross.

   _____

   b. The flag has dimensions 60 cm by 60 cm. Find the area of the red region.

   _____

TEST PREP

11. What is the area of the figure?

8 m
12 m   6 m

A 72 m²

B 102 m²

C 120 m²

D 144 m²

12. The area of a rectangle is 120 m². The length of the rectangle is 15 m. What is the width?

F 1,800 m   **H** 8 m

G 105 m   **J** 7 m

 PI AND CIRCUMFERENCE

There are three measurements that can be used to describe the size of a circle. The **diameter** of a circle is the distance across the circle through its center. The **radius** is the distance from the center to any point on the circle. The perimeter of a circle is the **circumference**.

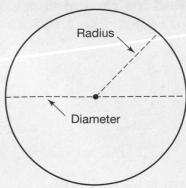

The diameter of a circle is twice its radius: $d = 2 \times r$.

The circumference of a circle is given by

$C = \pi \times d = 2 \times \pi \times r$.

The value for π is approximately equal to **3.14**, or $\frac{22}{7}$.

Example

Find the diameter and circumference of the circle. Use 3.14 for π.

The radius of the circle is 3 m.

The diameter is equal to two times the radius, so the diameter is 2×3, or 6 m.

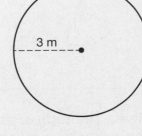

Use the formula to find the circumference. $C = 2 \times \pi \times r$

Substitute. $\approx 2 \times 3.14 \times 3$

Multiply. ≈ 18.84

The circumference is about **18.84 m.**

GUIDED PRACTICE

Find the radius and circumference of the circle.

1. **a.** What is the diameter? _____

   b. What is the radius? _____

   c. Substitute for the diameter and π in the formula

   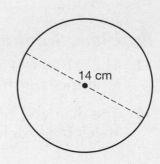

   $C = \pi \times d$. Use $\frac{22}{7}$ for π. _____

   d. What is the circumference? _____

Find the diameter and radius of a circle with a circumference of 28.26 ft.

2. **a.** Substitute for the circumference and π in the formula $C = \pi \times d$.
   $C = 28.26$ ft. Use 3.14 for π. _____

   b. What is the diameter? _____

   c. What is the radius? _____

NOW YOU TRY IT!

Find the circumference of each circle given the diameter
or radius. Use 3.14 for π.

1.

6 in.

_____

2.

18 cm

_____

3.

21 ft

_____

Find the circumference of each circle given the diameter
or radius. Use $\pi \approx \frac{22}{7}$. Express answers in lowest terms.

4.

7 m

_____

5.

$8\frac{1}{4}$ ft

_____

6.

14 km

_____

Given the radius, diameter, or circumference of a circle, find
the other two measurements. Use π ≈ 3.14. Round answers to
the nearest tenth.

7. $r =$ _____

    $d = 44$ cm

    $C \approx$ _____

8. $r =$ _____

    $d =$ _____

    $C = 4\pi$ cm

9. $r = 9$ mm

    $d =$ _____

    $C \approx$ _____

10. $r =$ _____

    $d = 6.8$ mi

    $C \approx$ _____

Problem Solving

11. The radius of Pluto is about 1,145 km.
Find the length of Pluto's equator.   _____

12. The diameter of a circular track at the park is 25 meters.
Haley ran around the track one time. How far did she run? _____

 LITTLE SOMETHING DIFFERENT...

Make calculations involving Earth.

The Earth's equator has a radius of approximately 3,959 mi.

a. Find the diameter of the earth.

_____

b. Find the circumference of the earth's
equator. Round to the nearest tenth.

_____

c. The diameter of the moon is 1,080.5 mi.
About how much larger is the
circumference of Earth than the moon?

_____

AREA OF CIRCLES

The circumference and the diameter of a circle are related by the number π. The radius and the area of a circle are also related by the number π. If you know the radius of a circle, you can use π to find the area.

$$\text{Area} = \pi \times r^2, \text{ where } r \text{ is the radius.}$$

Example 1

Find the area of this circle. Use 3.14 for π.

Use the formula $A = \pi \times r^2$.

Substitute 10 for r, the radius, and 3.14 for π.

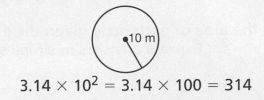

$$3.14 \times 10^2 = 3.14 \times 100 = 314$$

The area is 314 square meters, or 314 m^2.

Example 2

Given the area of a circle, find the radius.

$A = 200.96$ m^2

Use the formula $A = \pi \times r^2$.

Substitute 200.96 for the area, A, and 3.14 for π.

$$200.96 = 3.14 \times r^2$$
$$\frac{200.96}{3.14} = r^2$$
$$64 = r^2$$

The radius is 8 m.

$$8 = r$$

GUIDED PRACTICE

Find the area of each circle. Use 3.14 for π.

1.

3 in.

2.

4 ft

3.
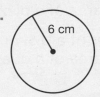
6 cm

_____   _____   _____

Given the area of a circle, find the radius or diameter. Use 3.14 for π.

4. $A = 153.86$ in^2

Think: $r^2 = 153.86 \div 3.14 =$ _____

$r =$ _____ in.

5. $A = 452.16$ m^2

Think: $r^2 = 452.16 \div 3.14 =$ _____

$r =$ _____ m;

$d =$ _____ m

NOW YOU TRY IT!

Find the area of each circle given the diameter or radius.
Use 3.14 for π.

1.

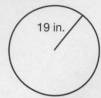

19 in.

_____

2.

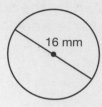

16 mm

_____

3.

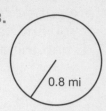

0.8 mi

_____

Find the area of each circle given the diameter or radius.
Use $\pi \approx \frac{22}{7}$. Express answers in simplest form.

4.

$8\frac{1}{2}$ ft

_____

5.

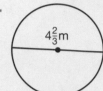

$4\frac{2}{3}$ m

_____

6.

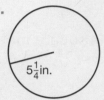

$5\frac{1}{4}$ in.

_____

Given the area of a circle, find the radius or diameter.
Use $\pi \approx 3.14$. Round answers to the nearest tenth.

7. $A \approx 31{,}400$ in^2

$r \approx$ _____

8. $A \approx 113.04$ cm^2

$d \approx$ _____

9. $A \approx 379.94$ mi^2

$r \approx$ _____

Problem Solving

Round answers to the nearest tenth.

10. Find the area of a pizza if the diameter is 15 in.   _____

11. The radius of a U.S. quarter is about 12 mm.
Find the area of a quarter.   _____

TEST PREP

12. The diameter of a speaker is 14 in.
Find the area of the speaker
rounded to the nearest tenth.

A 21.9 in^2

B 43.9 in^2

C 153.9 in^2

D 615.4 in^2

14 in.

13. Which parallelogram has the
greatest area?

F $h = 3.4$ m, $b = 2.8$ m

G $h = 2.8$ m, $b = 3.4$ m

H $h = 4$ m, $b = 3$ m

J $h = 5$ m, $b = 2$ m

TEST PREP

Circle each correct answer.

1. What is the area of the triangle?
   A 9.1 m²
   B 9.44 m²
   C 11.52 m²
   D 18.88 m²

   5.9 m
   3.2 m

2. The diameter of a circle is 14 m. What is the circumference? Use 3.14 for π.
   F 21.98 m   H 87.92 m
   G 43.96 m   J 153.86 m

3. The length of each side of a square is 58 in. What is the perimeter of the square?
   A 116 in.   C 232 in.
   B 174 in.   D 3,364 in.

4. What is the sin ∠A when the hypotenuse measures 30 m and the opposite leg measures 15 m?
   F 0.25   H 0.33
   G 0.5   J 2

5. What is the area of the trapezoid?
   A 115 ft²
   B 230 ft²
   C 630 ft²
   D 1,260 ft²

   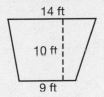
   14 ft
   10 ft
   9 ft

6. What is the area of the circle? Use 3.14 for π.
   F 25.12 cm²
   G 50.24 cm²
   H 200.96 cm²
   J 803.84 cm²

   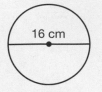
   16 cm

7. Square floor tiles often have an area of 929 cm². What is the length of a side of one of these tiles?
   A about 465   C about 90
   B about 232   D about 30

8. What is the area of the figure?
   F 35 in²
   G 42 in²
   H 150 in²
   J 156 in²

   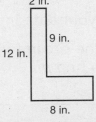
   2 in.
   9 in.
   12 in.
   8 in.

9. A map showed an area 25 mi by 25 mi. How many square miles were shown on the map?
   A 100 mi²   C 312.5 mi²
   B 125 mi²   D 625 mi²

10. What is the value of u?

    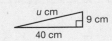
    u cm
    9 cm
    40 cm

    F 31   H 41
    G 40   J 49

SOMETHING DIFFERENT...

DISCOVERING PI

Pi is one of the oldest numbers, it was even known to the ancient Egyptians and Babylonians. Pi is different from many of the numbers that we use on daily basis because it is a non-repeating infinite decimal. This means that there is an infinite number of digits to the right of the decimal point in pi that never form a pattern. Computers have been able to calculate pi out to 50,000th place. In order to make pi more manageable it is typically written out to the hundredths as 3.14.

1. Measure the diameter of each of the coins. Use the diameter to find the radius of the coin.

2. Use a piece of string to measure the circumference of each coin.

3. Record your data into the table below.

4. Divide the circumference of each coin by the diameter in order to find *pi*.

	Silver Dollar	Quarter	Dime	Nickel	Penny
Diameter					
Circumference					
$\frac{C}{d}$					

SURFACE AREA OF PRISMS

The **surface area (SA)** of a prism is the sum of the areas of all of the faces. A **net** is a flat pattern that can be folded into a solid. To find the surface area of a prism such as this rectangular prism, unfold it into a net of polygons and then add each area.

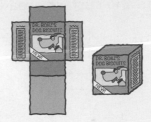

Like the area for a single polygon, surface area is measured in square units, such as cm².

Example

Find the surface area of the prism.

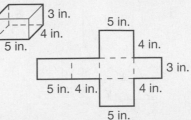

The net consists of two rectangles with lengths of 5 in. and widths of 4 in., two 4 in.-by-3 in. rectangles, and two 5 in.-by-3 in. rectangles.

SA = area of 2 rectangles + area of 2 rectangles + area of 2 rectangles

SA = 2 × (5 × 4)	+ 2 × (4 × 3)	+ 2 × (5 × 3)
= 2 × (20)	+ 2 × (12)	+ 2 × (15)
= 40	+ 24	+ 30
= 94 in²		

The surface area of the rectangular prism is 94 in².

GUIDED PRACTICE

Find the surface area of the prism.

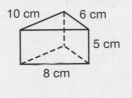
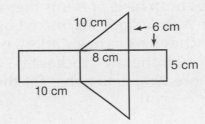

1. **a.** Which polygons make up the net?

   _____

   b. SA = area of + area of + area of + area of
            = rectangle   rectangle   rectangle   2 triangles

   = (___ × ___) + (___ × ___) + (___ × ___) + 2 × (___ × ___ ÷ 2)

   = ____ + ____ + ____ + ____

   = _____ cm²

2. 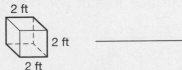   2 ft   2 ft   2 ft   _____

3.   5 m   1 m   1 m   _____

NOW YOU TRY IT!

Find the surface area of each prism.

1.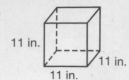
11 in. 11 in. 11 in.

2.
5 cm 13 cm 8 cm

3.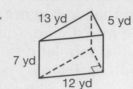
13 yd 5 yd 7 yd 12 yd

4.
23 mm 23 mm 23 mm

_____

5.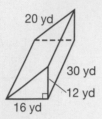
20 yd 30 yd 12 yd 16 yd

6.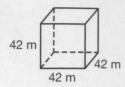
42 m 42 m 42 m

7.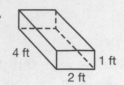
4 ft 1 ft 2 ft

8.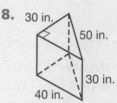
30 in. 50 in. 30 in. 40 in.

_____

Problem Solving

9. A music company wants to design a cardboard box for mailing a 2-CD set measuring 14.2 cm by 12.4 cm by 2.5 cm. What amount of surface area will the box have?

_____

10. A cereal box measures 16 cm by 6 cm by 25 cm. What is the surface area of the box?

_____

11. Wendy and Carlos both have presents they would like to gift wrap. Wendy's gift fits into a box that is 8 inches by 7 inches by 3 inches. Carlos's gift fits into a box that is 10 inches by 4 inches by 3 inches. Who will need more wrapping paper for their gift?

_____

A LITTLE SOMETHING DIFFERENT...

Make a skateboarding ramp. Find the surface area.

a. On paper, sketch the net below. Fill the whole page.

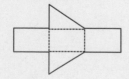

b. Cut out the shape. Fold it along the black lines to make a three dimensional ramp.

c. Measure the sides of your figure to the nearest inch.

d. What is the surface area of your ramp?

_____

SKILL 17 SURFACE AREA OF CYLINDERS

All of the faces of a prism are flat. Other three-dimensional objects have circular faces and curved sides. A **cylinder** has two parallel circular bases with the same radius.

You can use a net to see shapes and dimensions of the faces. Then you can use area formulas to calculate surface areas.

Example

Find the surface area of the cylinder. Use π = 3.14.

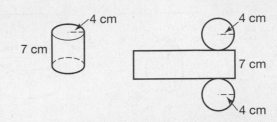

Find the area of each part of the net.
First, find the area of each circle.

$A = π × r^2 = 3.14 × 4^2 = 3.14 × 4 × 4 ≈ 50.24 \text{ cm}^2$

The length of the rectangle is equal to the circumference of the circle.

$C = 2 × π × r = 2 × 3.14 × 4 = 25.12 \text{ cm}$

The width of the rectangle is equal to the height of the cylinder, 7.
Multiply 25.12 by 7.

$A = 25.12 × 7 = 175.84 \text{ cm}^2$

Add the areas to find the surface area.

$(2 × 50.24)\text{cm}^2 + 175.84 \text{ cm}^2 = 276.32 \text{ cm}^2$

So, the surface area of the cylinder is 276.32 cm².

GUIDED PRACTICE

Find the surface area of the cylinder. Use π = 3.14.

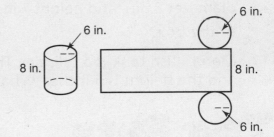

1. Area of each base = $π × r^2$

    = 3.14 × _____

    = 3.14 × _____

    = _____ in²

2. Length of rectangle (circumference of circle) = $2 × π × r$

    = 2 × 3.14 × _____

    = _____

3. Width of the rectangle = _____

4. Area of the rectangle = length × width = _____ × _____ = _____ in²

5. Surface area of the cylinder = area of both bases + area of rectangle

    = (_____ × 113.04) + _____

    = _____ in²

NOW YOU TRY IT!

Find the surface area of each cylinder. Use 3.14 for π.

1. 6 ft 32 ft

_____

2. 6 in. 12 in.

_____

3. 4 m 9 m

_____

4. 7 cm 17 cm

_____

5. 1.6 m 1.8 m

_____

6. 7 yd 6 yd

_____

7. $3\frac{3}{4}$ in. 8 in.

_____

8. 41 cm 98 cm

_____

Given the radius and height of each cylinder, find the surface area (SA). Use 3.14 for π. Round to the nearest whole number.

9. $r = 3.8$ ft, $h = 15$ ft

$SA \approx$ _____

10. $r = 21$ m, $h = 4$ m

$SA \approx$ _____

11. $r = 12$ in., $h = 13$ in.

$SA \approx$ _____

Problem Solving

Round to the nearest whole number.

12. An oatmeal box has the shape of a cylinder with diameter $3\frac{7}{8}$ in. and height 7 in. What is the surface area of the box?

_____

13. Maria's fish tank is a cylinder. The diameter is 14 inches and the height is 5 inches. What is the surface area?

_____

TEST PREP

14. What is the surface area of the cylinder? Use 3.14 for π.

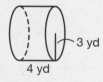
3 yd 4 yd

A 75.36 yd²   **C** 103.62 yd²

B 131.88 yd²   **D** 150.72 yd²

15. What is the surface area of the prism?

3 cm 2 cm 1 cm

F 6 cm²   **H** 18 cm²

G 11 cm²   **J** 22 cm²

SKILL 18 — VOLUME OF RECTANGULAR PRISMS

The **volume** is the number of cubic units in a solid. The volume of this solid is 1 cm³.

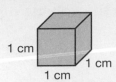

1 cm
1 cm
1 cm

The volume of a rectangular prism is found by multiplying the area of the base (*B*) times the height (*h*) of the prism. Remember that the area of the base is length × width.

$V = B \times h$ or
$V = l \times w \times h$

Example 1

Find the volume of the rectangular prism shown.

Step 1: Find the area of the rectangular base.

$B = 4 \times 7 = 28 \text{ in}^2$

Step 2: Find the volume.

$V = B \times h = 28 \times 5 = 140 \text{ in}^3$

So, the volume of the rectangular prism is 140 in³.

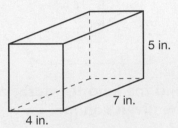

5 in.
7 in.
4 in.

Example 2

Find the height of the rectangular prism with volume 225 cm³ and base dimensions 5 cm by 5 cm.

Step 1: Find the area of the rectangular base.

$B = 5 \times 5 = 25 \text{ cm}^2$

Step 2: Substitute in the volume formula to find the height.

$V = B \times h \qquad 225 = 25 \times h$
$\qquad\qquad\qquad\qquad\quad 9 = h$

So, the height of the rectangular prism is 9 cm.

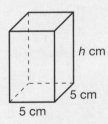

h cm
5 cm
5 cm

GUIDED PRACTICE

1. **Find the volume of the rectangular prism.**

   a. Find the area of the base. _____

   b. Find the volume. _____

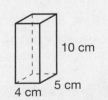

10 cm
4 cm
5 cm

2. **Find the height of the figure. The volume is 960 in³.**

   a. Find the area of the base. _____

   b. Substitute in the volume formula to find the height. _____

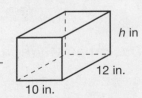

h in
12 in.
10 in.

NOW YOU TRY IT!

Find the volume of each rectangular prism.

1.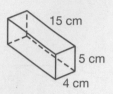
5 cm
17 cm
6 cm

_____

2.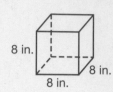
4 in.
5 in.
5 in.

_____

3.
2 m
7 m
8 m

_____

4.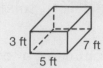
3 ft
7 ft
5 ft

_____

5.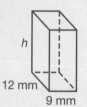
15 cm
5 cm
4 cm

_____

6.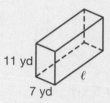
8 in.
8 in.
8 in.

_____

7.
3 m
16 m
16 m

_____

8.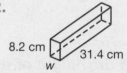
3 yd
3 yd
8 yd

_____

Find the length, width, or height of the rectangular prism with the given volume.

9.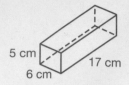
h
12 mm
9 mm

$V = 3{,}024 \text{ mm}^3$

h = _____

10.
11 yd
7 yd
ℓ

$V = 1{,}540 \text{ yd}^3$

l = _____

11.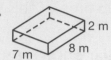
6 in.
h
$2\frac{1}{4}$ in.

$V = 50\frac{5}{8} \text{ in}^3$

h = _____

12.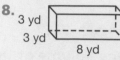
8.2 cm
31.4 cm
w

$V = 1{,}338.896 \text{ cm}^3$

w = _____

Problem Solving

13. The Panama Canal has a length of 89,200 yd, a width of 37 yd, and a depth of 14 yd. Estimate the volume of water in the canal by assuming it has the shape of a rectangular prism.

_____

14. The freezer compartment in a refrigerator is 20 in. long, 16 in. wide, and 11 in. deep. What is the volume of the freezer compartment?

_____

A LITTLE SOMETHING DIFFERENT...

Design an Olympic swimming pool.

a. The Olympic Swimming Pool in the 2000 Olympics was 50 m × 25 m × 3 m.

b. What was the volume of the pool?

c. Design your own swimming pool on a separate sheet of paper. Find the volume.

_____

VOLUME OF TRIANGULAR PRISMS AND CYLINDERS

The volume of prisms and cylinders is the product of the area of the base (*B*) and the height (*h*).

Example 1

Find the volume of the triangular prism.

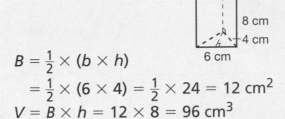

Step 1: Find the area of the base. Use the formula for area of a triangle.

$$B = \frac{1}{2} \times (b \times h)$$
$$= \frac{1}{2} \times (6 \times 4) = \frac{1}{2} \times 24 = 12 \text{ cm}^2$$
$$V = B \times h = 12 \times 8 = 96 \text{ cm}^3$$

Step 2: Find the volume.

The volume of the triangular prism is 96 cm³.

Example 2

Find the volume of the cylinder.

Step 1: Find the area of the base. Use the formula for area of a circle. Use 3.14 for π

$$B = \pi \times r^2$$
$$= 3.14 \times 10^2 = 3.14 \times 100 = 314 \text{ in}^2$$
$$V = B \times h = 314 \times 5 = 1{,}570 \text{ in}^3$$

Step 2: Find the volume.

The volume of the cylinder is 1,570 in³.

GUIDED PRACTICE

Find the volume of the triangular prism.

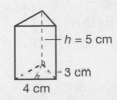

1. **a.** What figure is the base? _____

    b. What is the area of the base? _____

    c. What is the prism's height? _____

    d. What is its volume? _____

Find the volume of the cylinder. Use 3.14 for π.

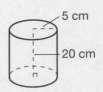

2. **a.** What figure is the base? _____

    b. What is the area of the base? _____

    c. What is the height? _____

    d. What is the volume? _____

NOW YOU TRY IT!

Find the volume of each solid. Use 3.14 for π. Round each answer to a whole number.

1.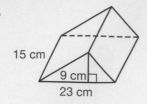

15 cm
9 cm
23 cm

_____

2.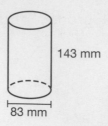

143 mm

83 mm

_____

3.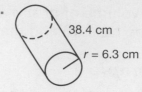

38.4 cm
r = 6.3 cm

_____

4.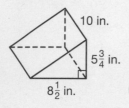

10 in.
$5\frac{3}{4}$ in.
$8\frac{1}{2}$ in.

_____

5.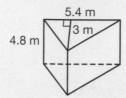

5.4 m
3 m
4.8 m

_____

6.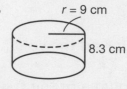

r = 9 cm
8.3 cm

_____

7.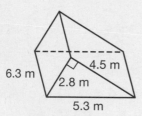

4.5 m
6.3 m
2.8 m
5.3 m

_____

8.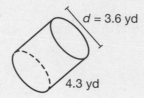

d = 3.6 yd
4.3 yd

_____

9.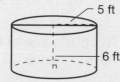

5 ft
6 ft

_____

Problem Solving

10. The attic of Karen's house has the shape of the triangular prism shown at the right. Find the volume of the attic.

9 ft 45 ft
30 ft

_____

11. A cylindrical cookie tin has a diameter of 10 in. and a height of $3\frac{1}{2}$ in. How many cubic inches of cookies can it hold? Round your answer to the nearest cubic inch.

_____

TEST PREP

12. Find the volume of the cylinder. Use 3.14 for π.

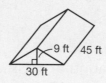

2 cm
4 cm

A 37.68 cm³   **C** 75.36 cm³

B 50.24 cm³   **D** 100.48 cm³

13. What is the volume of a cube that has sides of length 7 cm?

F 343 cm³   **H** 98 cm³

G 294 cm³   **J** 49 cm³

PROBLEM SOLVING: CHOOSING BETWEEN SURFACE AREA AND VOLUME

When solving word problems involving surface area and volume, it is important to ask yourself whether you are filling up or covering the solid.

Example

A can of dog food has diameter 7.4 cm and height 10.3 cm. How much metal was used to make the can?

Read   The diameter of the can is 7.4 cm, and the height is 10.3 cm.

Plan   You are asked how much metal it would take to make the can, not how much it takes to fill the can. So, find the surface area.

Solve   Find the surface area. The radius of the can is 3.7 cm. Find the areas of the 2 congruent circular bases:

$$2 \times \text{area of 1 circle} = 2 \times \pi \times r^2$$
$$\approx 2 \times 3.14 \times 3.7^2$$
$$= 85.9732 \text{ cm}^2$$

Find the area of the curved side of the can:

$$\text{circumference of base} \times \text{height} = 2 \times \pi \times r^2 \times h^2$$
$$\approx 2 \times 3.14 \times 3.7 \times 10.3$$
$$= 239.3308 \text{ cm}^2$$

Add the areas: $85.9732 \text{ cm}^2 + 239.3308 \text{ cm}^2 = 325.304 \text{ cm}^2$

It takes about 325.3 cm^2 of metal to make the can.

Look Back See whether your answer makes sense. The areas of both circular bases and the area of the curved side were used. The multiplication and addition are correct. So, the answer seems to be the correct surface area.

GUIDED PRACTICE

1. The tunnel on Yerba Buena Island near San Francisco, California, is about 78 ft wide, 56 ft tall, and 540 ft long. Find the amount of air in the tunnel by assuming that the tunnel has the shape of a rectangular prism.

   a. Will you find surface area or volume? _____

   b. What dimensions are you given?

   _____

   c. What equation for rectangular prisms can you use? _____

   d. What is the amount of air in the tunnel? _____

1. Juan is wrapping a box that contains a surprise gift for his mother. The box is 9 in. long, 7 in. wide, and 3 in. tall. How much wrapping paper will he use if he cuts paper to exactly fit the sides of the box?

2. At a winter festival, a city hires local artists to make ice sculptures. One artist started with a block of ice 6 ft tall, 3 ft wide, and 3 ft long. She chipped away $\frac{1}{3}$ of the ice to make a polar bear. How much ice was in the polar bear itself?

3. A pool for water lilies has the shape of a rectangular prism 10 ft long, 4 ft wide, and 4 ft deep. How much water can the pool hold?

4. A box of shredded wheat cereal measures 7 in. by 10 in. by 2 in. How much cardboard is used for the box? (Assume no overlap.)

5. Doreen has a large sandbox that holds twice the amount of sand that her small sandbox will hold. The small sandbox is 3 ft by $2\frac{1}{2}$ ft by 1 ft. How much sand can the large sandbox hold when filled level to the top?

6. A stick of butter is shaped like a rectangular prism. The stick of butter is 5 in. long, $1\frac{1}{2}$ in. wide, and $1\frac{1}{2}$ in. thick. How much butter does the stick contain?

7. A rectangular box with no top is 7 in. long, 5 in. wide, and 3 in. deep. If Hector paints the outside of the box (sides and bottom) with gold paint, what is the measure of what he will paint?

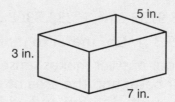

A LITTLE SOMETHING DIFFERENT...

Solve the riddle.

Determine whether you would use surface area or volume in each example. Write the correct term on the line. Then, use the letters from each word to find the answer.

1. Foil around a burrito

   _____ (1st letter)

2. Filling a bottle _____ (2nd letter)

3. Filling a watering can _____ (3rd letter)

4. Painting a toy _____ _____ (5th letter)

5. Wrapping a gift _____ _____ (3rd letter)

What system is in the sky?

____ ____ ____ ____ ____
 1   2   3   4   5

SKILL 21 CONNECTING VOLUME, MASS, AND CAPACITY

One liter fills 1,000 cm³ of space.
In science, you learn that the mass of 1 cm³ of water is 1 g (1 gram).

Example

What is the mass of the water that the aquarium can hold?

Step 1: Find the volume.

20 cm × 20 cm × 40 cm = 16,000 cm³

Step 2: Change cm³ to mL.

1 cm³ holds 1 mL.

So, 16,000 cm³ holds 16,000 mL.

Step 3: Change mL to g.

1 mL of water has a mass of 1 g.

So, 16,000 mL has a mass of 16,000 g.

Step 4: Change g to kg.

1 kg = 1,000 g.

So, 16,000 g = 16,000 ÷ 1,000 = 16 kg.

The mass of the water the aquarium will hold is 16 kg.

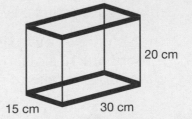

GUIDED PRACTICE

Find the mass, in kilograms, of the water the aquarium can hold.

1. **a.** Find the volume. _____

   b. Change cm³ to mL. _____

   c. Change mL to g. _____

   d. Change g to kg. _____

Complete each sentence.

2. A 1,000 cm³ container holds _____ mL of water, which is _____ L.

3. 1 L of water has a mass of _____ g, which is _____ kg.

4. A 3,000 cm³ container holds _____ mL of water, which is _____ L.

5. 2,000 mL of water fills a _____ cm³ container.

6. 25 L of water has a mass of _____ g, which is _____ kg.

7. 2 kg of water has a volume of _____ L.

NOW YOU TRY IT!

Complete the table.

	Volume (cm³)	Amount of water (L)	Amount of water (mL)	Mass of water (kg)	Mass of water (g)
1. **Aquarium A**			25,000		
2. **Aquarium B**	1,800				
3. **Aquarium C**		120			
4. **Aquarium D**				44.6	

Complete each sentence.

5. 1,800 mL of water would fill a(n) _____ cm³ container.

6. 2.9 kg of water would fill a(n) _____ mL container.

7. 1.25 L of water has a mass of _____ kg.

8. A 50 cm³ container can hold _____ L.

Problem Solving

Solve each problem.

9. A bucket and the water in it have a combined mass of 5 kg. If you put enough additional water in the bucket to increase the combined mass to 5.3 kg, how many liters of water have you added? _____

10. A drinking glass contains 210 grams of water. How many cubic centimeters of water are in the glass? _____

11. The volume of each slot of an ice cube tray is 30 cm³. If there are 16 slots in one tray, how many grams of liquid water does it take to fill one tray? _____

TEST PREP

12. Mark is going to carry a bottle of water on a camping trip. If he fills the bottle with 0.75 L of water, how much mass does the water itself add to the mass of his backpack?

   A 75 g   **C** 75 kg

   B 750 g   **D** 750 kg

13. How much wood do you paint if you paint the outside of a closed, rectangular wooden box that is 40 cm by 30 cm by 25 cm?

   F 95 cm³   **H** 5,900 cm²

   G 2,950 cm²   **J** 30,000 cm³

SECTION C WRAP-UP

TEST PREP

Circle each correct answer.

1. How much ice is in a rectangular block of ice 14 in. by 15 in. by 20 in.?

A 790 in^2 **C** 1,580 in^2

B 1,020 in^3 **D** 4,200 in^3

2. What is the surface area of the rectangular prism?

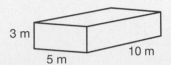

F 190 m^2 **H** 95 m^2

G 150 m^2 **J** 75 m^2

3. What is the volume of the triangular prism?

A 72 m^3

B 108 m^3

C 216 m^3

D 432 m^3

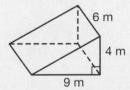

4. What is the surface area of the cylinder? Use 3.14 for π.

F 200 in^2

G 1,000 in^2

H 1,334.5 in^2

J 1,413 in^2

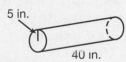

5. What is the mass in kilograms of 2,500 cm^3 of water?

A 2.5 kg   **C** 250 kg

B 25 kg   **D** 2,500 kg

6. What is the volume of a rectangular prism that is 7 in. long, 6 in. wide, and 8.5 in. tall?

F 357 in^3 **H** 221 in^3

G 305 in^3 **J** 203 in^3

7. What is the surface area of the triangular prism?

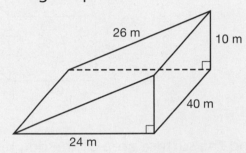

A 3,024 m^2 **C** 2,500 m^2

B 2,640 m^2 **D** 2,400 m^2

8. What is the volume of the cylinder? Use 3.14 for π.

F 3,140 cm^3

G 5,024 cm^3

H 40,000 cm^3

J 125,600 cm^3

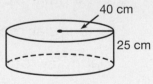

9. A rectangular prism measures 9 cm by 5 cm by 2 cm. Find the volume.

A 45 cm^3 **C** 90 cm^3

B 73 cm^3 **D** 146 cm^3

10. Find the surface area for the rectangular prism from question 9.

F 73 cm^2 **H** 146 cm^2

G 90 cm^2 **J** 292 cm^2

SOMETHING DIFFERENT...

IN THE DOGHOUSE BUSINESS

You and a friend are thinking about going into business building doghouses. First you need to know a few things about what kinds of materials you are going to need.

The diagram below shows some of the dimensions of the doghouse you are going to build.

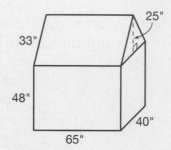

1. Find the surface area of the dog house and how much paint you will need. Think about each shape in doghouse and then add them together to get a total surface area. Use the list below.

   2 rectangular side walls _____

   2 rectangular front and back walls _____

   2 rectangular roof panels _____

   2 triangular roof panels _____

   Total Surface Area of the doghouse: _____

2. How much space is there inside the doghouse? Calculate the volume of the doghouse. Consider that the doghouse is a rectangular prism and a triangular prism. Show your work.

   _____

   _____

   _____

SKILL 22 — EXPLORING POLYHEDRONS

Three-dimensional objects take up space. A three-dimensional object, or **solid**, whose **faces** are polygons is a **polyhedron**. The segments joining the faces are **edges,** and the corners are **vertices.** Hidden edges in three-dimensional figure are shown as dashed lines.

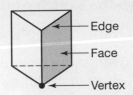

Edge
Face
Vertex

A **prism** is a polyhedron whose **bases** are congruent and parallel. A **pyramid** has a polygonal base but comes to a point. The name of a prism or pyramid tells the shape of its base.

Rectangular prism **Square** pyramid **Hexagonal** prism

Example

Name the polyhedron.

The solid has two congruent parallel bases, so it is a prism.

The base is a triangle.

The solid is a triangular prism.

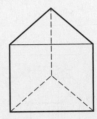

GUIDED PRACTICE

Name each polyhedron.

a. Does Polyhedron *A* have two congruent bases or does it have a polygonal base opposite a point?

_____

b. Is Polyhedron *A* a prism or a pyramid? _____

c. What shape is the base of Polyhedron *A*? _____

d. Name Polyhedron *A*. _____

e. Does Polyhedron *B* have two congruent bases or does it have a polygonal base opposite a point?

_____

f. Is Polyhedron *B* a prism or a pyramid? _____

g. What shape is the base of Polyhedron *B*? _____

h. Name Polyhedron *B*? _____

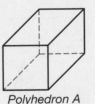

Polyhedron A

Polyhedron B

i.

j.

_____ _____

NOW YOU TRY IT!

Use the sketch of the polyhedron to answer each question.

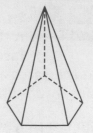

1. Name the polyhedron. _____

2. Name the polygons that are the faces of the polyhedron. How many of each type of polygon are there?

   _____

3. How many edges, faces, and vertices does the polyhedron have?

   Edges: _____   Faces: _____   Vertices: _____

Name each polyhedron.

4. _____

   _____

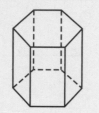

5. _____

   _____

6. _____

   _____

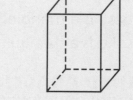

7. _____

   _____

8. _____

   _____

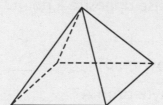

9. _____

   _____

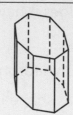

Problem Solving

10. A new building is a pentagonal prism. If the outside walls of the building are being painted, how many faces are being painted?   _____

    How many faces does a pentagonal prism have total?   _____

TEST PREP

11. How many faces does the figure have?

    A 2   **C** 7

    B 5   **D** 10

12. What is the volume of a cube that has sides of length 7 cm?

    F 343 cm³   **H** 98 cm³

    G 294 cm³   **J** 49 cm³

50   © by Pearson Education, Inc., publishing as Pearson Prentice Hall

PERSPECTIVE

A sketch can help you visualize a 3-D object. If a shape is made of cubes, draw a base plan to show the height of several stacks of cubes.

Example 1

Draw a base plan of the 3-D object shown.

There are two columns that are 3 cubes high.
There are two columns that are 2 cubes high.
There are two columns that are 1 cube high.

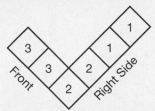

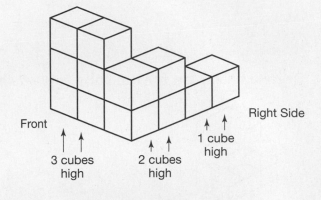

Example 2

Draw the right, front, and top view for the 3-D object shown.

The front has one stack of 3 cubes and one stack of 2 cubes and one stack of 1 cube.

The right has two stacks of 2 cubes and one stack of 1 cube.

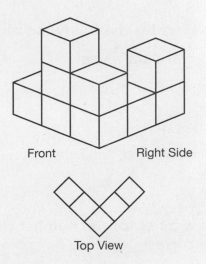

Right View   Front View   Top View

GUIDED PRACTICE

1. **Draw a base plan of the 3-D object shown.**

   a.

   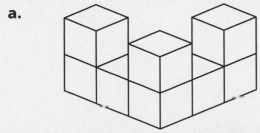

2. **Draw the right, front, and top view for the 3-D object shown.**

   a.

   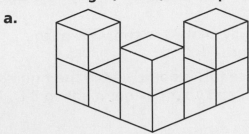

1. Draw the right, front, and top views for the 3-D object shown.

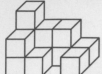

Draw a base plan for the cube towers shown.

2.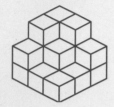

3.

Draw a net for the following objects:

4. a rectangular prism

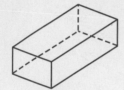

5. a regular triangular prism

6. Draw a net for the number cube shown. Show the dots in the correct position.

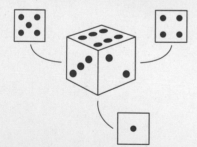

A LITTLE SOMETHING DIFFERENT...

With a partner, use your graph paper to create different views of 3-D objects.

a. With your graph paper, construct the front view of a figure.

b. Now, make the right view of it.

c. Finally, make the top view of the object.

d. Once this is done, sketch the figures you and your partner made in 3-D.

SKILL 24 ISOMETRIC AND ORTHOGRAPHIC DRAWING

Isometric drawing is one method used to give perspective to a drawing. Using isometric dot paper makes isometric drawing easier. However, the angles may be distorted.

Orthographic drawing shows angles and lengths accurately. In an orthographic view, you look directly at the object from front, side, and top views.

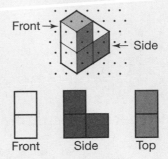

Example

Match the isometric drawing with a set of orthographic views.

Compare the heights of the stacks. The tallest stack in the isometric drawing is two cubes high, so the side and front orthographic views should also have stacks with two cubes.

Determine that the number of cubes and their position is correct in each view. There should be 4 cubes in the side and top views and 3 cubes in the front view. View **A** has the correct number and placement of cubes.

Set **A** matches the isometric drawing.

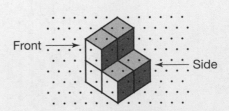

GUIDED PRACTICE

Match each isometric drawing with a set of orthographic views.

1. How many cubes high is Drawing *A*? _____

2. How many cubes would be viewed from the front of Drawing *A*? _____

3. How many cubes would be viewed from the side of Drawing *A*? _____

4. How many cubes would be viewed from the top of Drawing *A*? _____

5. Which set of orthographic views correctly represents Drawing *A*? _____

6. How many cubes high is Drawing *B*? _____

7. How many cubes would be viewed from the front of Drawing *B*? _____

8. How many cubes would be viewed from the side of Drawing *B*? _____

9. How many cubes would be viewed from the top of Drawing *B*? _____

10. Which set of orthographic views correctly represents Drawing *B*? _____

Find the number of cubes in each figure. Assume all cubes are visible.

1. _____

2. _____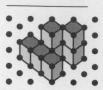

3. _____

4. _____

Match each isometric drawing with a set of orthographic views.

5. _____

6. _____

7. _____

8. _____

A.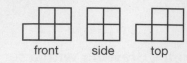
front   side   top

B.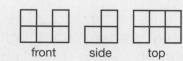
front   side   top

C.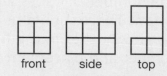
front   side   top

D.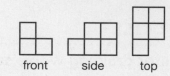
front   side   top

TEST PREP

9. How many cubes high is the figure?

A 0   C 3
B 2   D 5

10. How many vertices does a triangular prism have?

F 3   H 5
G 4   J 12

NAME _____ DATE _____

 **TRANSLATIONS**

When you change the position or size of a figure, you have performed a **transformation**. A **translation** is a transformation that slides a figure without changing its size or orientation.

You can also write a rule to describe the translation.

Example 1

Which lettered figure is a translation of ΔA?

Compare the size and orientation of each new triangle.

ΔB is a different size.

ΔC has a different orientation. It has been turned.

ΔD is the same size and same orientation.

So, ΔD is a translation of ΔA.

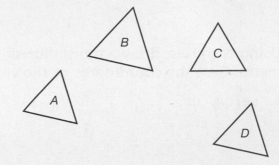

Example 2

Write a rule for the translation "left 3 up 2."

Remember that left and right show movement along the *x*-axis. Up and down show movement along the *y*-axis.

Left and down are negative directions. When a figure is moved left or down, you *subtract* from the original coordinates.

Right and up are positive directions. When a figure is moved right or up, you *add* to the original coordinates.

The rule "left 3, up 2" can be written as $(x, y) \rightarrow (x - 3, y + 2)$.

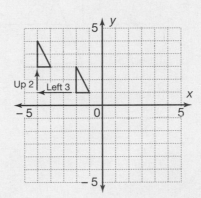

GUIDED PRACTICE

1. **Which lettered figure is a translation of Hexagon *E*?**

   a. Which figure is a different size? _____

   b. Which figures have a different orientation?

   _____

   c. Which figure is a translation? _____

2. **Write a rule for the translation "right 5, down 6."**

   a. Will you add to or subtract from the *x*-coordinate? _____

   b. Will you add to or subtract from the *y*-coordinate? _____

   c. Complete the rule. $(x, y) \rightarrow$ _____

NOW YOU TRY IT!

For each group of figures, identify all lettered polygons that are translations of the shaded polygon.

1. _____

2. _____
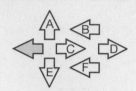

3. _____
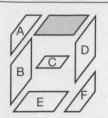

Using each rule, draw a translation of figure *QRST* on a coordinate plane. Give the coordinates of the vertices of the translation.

4. Left 4, up 2

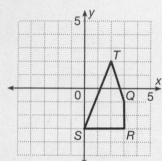

Q' _____   R' _____

S' _____   T' _____

5. $(x, y) \rightsquigarrow (x + 5, y + 3)$

Q' _____   R' _____

S' _____   T' _____

Problem Solving

6. The Japanese word shown at the right means "extensive forest." Circle the portions of this word that are translations of each other.

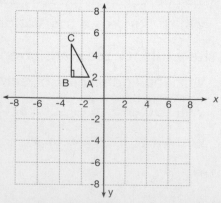

A LITTLE SOMETHING DIFFERENT...

Using the graph below, cast your net to try and tame the tiger by making translations.

a. First, use the triangle on the graph to represent your net. Note where its present points are, and move your net down 6, left one.

b. Oops! You missed the tiger. Cast your net again. This time, move it right 5 and up 3.

c. Almost! Give it one more try. This time, cast your net up 4 and right 2.

d. You've caught the tiger! Good job.

© by Pearson Education, Inc., publishing as Pearson Prentice Hall

SKILL 26 REFLECTIONS AND LINE SYMMETRY

When one half of an object is a mirror image of the other, the object has **line symmetry**, and the imaginary "mirror" is the **line of symmetry**.

The transformation created by flipping a figure is a **reflection**.

Example 1

Decide whether the figure has line symmetry. If so, draw each line.

The figure has **two lines of symmetry**.

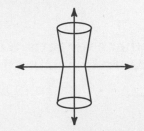

Example 2

Draw the reflection of △PQR across the y-axis and give the coordinates of its vertices.

To reflect each point, find the distance to the line of reflection. Go the same distance on the other side of the line and mark the reflection point.

Point P (−1, 6) is one unit to the *left* of the y-axis, so its reflection, P′ is one unit to the *right* of the y-axis at (1, 6).

Point Q (−3, 1) is three units to the *left* of the y-axis, so its reflection, Q′ is three units to the *right* of the y-axis at (3, 1).

Point R (−5, 3) is five units to the *left* of the y-axis, so its reflection, R′ is five units to the *right* of the y-axis at (5, 3).

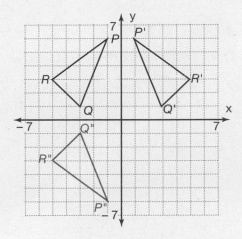

The coordinates of the vertices of the reflection are P′(1, 6), Q′(3, 1), and R′(5, 3).

GUIDED PRACTICE

1. Decide whether the figure has line symmetry. If so, draw each line.

   a.

   b.

   c.

2. Draw the reflection of △PQR across the x-axis and give the coordinates of its vertices.

   a. Will you move up, down, left, or right to reflect across the x-axis? _____

   b. What are the coordinates of each point?

      Point P″ _____   Point Q″ _____   Point R″ _____

NOW YOU TRY IT!

Decide whether each figure has line symmetry.
If it does, draw and number the lines of symmetry.

1. Parallelogram _____

2. Ellipse _____

3. Isosceles Trapezoid _____

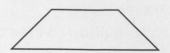

Decide whether each pattern or object has line symmetry.
If it does, draw and number the lines of symmetry.

4. _____

5. _____

6. _____

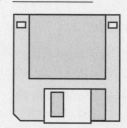

Draw each figure and its reflection on a coordinate plane.

7. △ABC with A(−3, 4), B(−1, 2) and C(−5, 1) reflected across the x-axis.

8. DEFG with D(−4, 0), E(−5, −4), F(−2, −3) and G(−1, −1), reflected across the y-axis

TEST PREP

9. How many line of symmetry does the figure have?

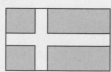

A 0

B 1

C 2

D 4

10. Point Q is positioned on (3, 2). The translation of Q has the coordinates (1, 5). What is the rule for the translation of point Q?

F down 2, right 3

H down 2, left 3

G up 2, left 3

J up 2, right 3

SKILL 27 ROTATIONS AND ROTATIONAL SYMMETRY

A **rotation** is a transformation that pivots a figure around a point.
A full turn is a 360° rotation.

| Original position | $\frac{1}{4}$ clockwise turn 90° clockwise rotation | $\frac{1}{2}$ clockwise turn 180° clockwise rotation | $\frac{3}{4}$ clockwise turn 270° clockwise rotation | Full turn 360° rotation |

A figure has **rotational symmetry** if a rotation of less than
360° rotates the figure onto itself.

Example 1

Decide whether the figure has rotational
symmetry. If it does, name all clockwise
fractional turns that rotate the figure onto itself.

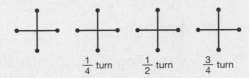

Imagine the figure rotating around its center.
Turn the figure until it rotates onto itself.

The figure has rotational symmetry. It overlaps at $\frac{1}{4}$ turn, $\frac{1}{2}$ turn,
and $\frac{3}{4}$ turn.

Example 2

Give the smallest fractional turn that each figure has been
rotated clockwise. Then express your answer in degrees.

Imagine the figure rotating around its center.

The figure has been rotated $\frac{1}{2}$ turn, which is a **180° rotation**.

GUIDED PRACTICE

1. Decide whether each figure has rotational symmetry. If it
   does, name all clockwise fractional turns that rotate the
   figure onto itself.

   a.   **b.** 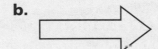   **c.**

   _____   _____   _____

2. Give the smallest fractional turn that each figure has been
   rotated clockwise. Then express your answer in degrees. If you
   need help, cut out the figure and turn it to see the overlaps.

   a.   **b.**   **c.**

   _____   _____   _____

NOW YOU TRY IT!

Give the smallest fractional turn that each figure has been
rotated clockwise. Express your answer in degrees.

1. Clock face _____

2. Dumb bell _____

3. Puerto Rican flag _____

 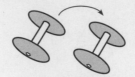 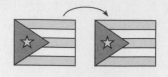

4. Give the coordinates of △PQR after clockwise rotations
around the origin of:

a. 90° ($\frac{1}{4}$ turn) P′ _____ Q′ _____ R′ _____

b. 180° ($\frac{1}{2}$ turn) P″ _____ Q″ _____ R″ _____

c. 270° ($\frac{3}{4}$ turn) P‴ _____ Q‴ _____ R‴ _____

d. 360° (full turn) P⁗ _____ Q⁗ _____ R⁗ _____

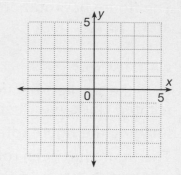

5. Draw rectangle *STUV* with *S*(0, 3), *T*(1, 4), *U*(3, 2) and *V*(2, 1).
Give the coordinates of rotations of *STUV* after clockwise
rotations of:

a. 90° ($\frac{1}{4}$ turn) S′ _____ T′ _____

U′ _____ V′ _____

b. 180° ($\frac{1}{2}$ turn) S″ _____ T′ _____

U″ _____ V″ _____

c. 270° ($\frac{3}{4}$ turn) S‴ _____ T‴ _____

U‴ _____ V‴ _____

d. 360° (full turn) S⁗ _____ T‴ _____

U⁗ _____ V⁗ _____

 LITTLE SOMETHING DIFFERENT...

**Work with a partner to take turns
rotating a figure on a coordinate plane.**

a. Use a spinner with ten sections. Label
two of the sections each of the
following: 90° turn, 180° turn, 270°
turn, 90° turn, and no change.

b. Use the coordinate plane to draw
a two-dimensional shape. Label each

vertex starting with the
letter A. What it the name of
your figure?

_____

c. Take turns with a friend to spin
and rotate the figure as instructed
at point A.

TEST PREP

Circle each correct answer.

1. How many vertices does a cube have?

   A 4   **C** 8

   B 6   **D** 12

2. What figure can be made from the net below?

   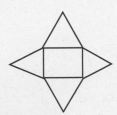

   F rectangular prism

   G trianglar prism

   H square pyramid

   J hexagonal pyramid

3. Which answer is the rule for the translation: right 2, down 3?

   A $(x + 2, y - 3)$ **C** $(x + 2, y + 3)$

   B $(y - 2, x - 2)$ **D** $(x + 3, y - 2)$

4. How many lines of symmetry does the figure contain?

   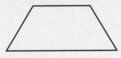

   F 0   **H** 2

   G 1   **J** 3

5. Which fractional turn will allow the figure to rotate onto itself?

   A $\frac{1}{2}$ turn   **C** $\frac{3}{4}$ turn

   B $\frac{1}{4}$ turn   **D** full turn

6. Classify the figure.

   F rectangular prism

   G octagonal prism

   H square pyramid

   J hexagonal prism

7. Point F is located at (3, 2). If the rule $(x - 4, y + 3)$ is applied to F, what are the new coordinates?

   A $(-2, 6)$ **C** $(7, 5)$

   B $(-1, 5)$ **D** $(1, 0)$

8. Use the side view below. How many cubes high is the front of the figure?

   F 2   **H** 5

   G 4   **J** 6

Use the drawing of Triangle EFG below to answer # 9 and 10.

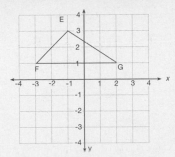

9. Where would point F be located if $\triangle$EFG was rotated $\frac{1}{4}$ turn at point G?

   A $(1, 7)$ **C** $(2, -4)$

   B $(1, -3)$ **D** $(2, 6)$

10. Where would point F be located in order to create a reflection of $\triangle$EFG across the *x*-axis?

    F $(-2, 3)$ **H** $(2, 3)$

    G $(2, -3)$ **J** $(3, -2)$

SOMETHING DIFFERENT...

TESSELLATIONS

A tessellation is an arrangement of congruent regular polygons in a repetive pattern. They are used in tile patterns, quilting patterns and art.

The pattern below is the tesselation of triangles.

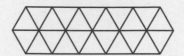

1. Draw the lines of symmetry that apply to the figure above.

2. The tesselation contains one equilateral triangle that has been rotated several times. Begin at the top left triangle and list all of the rotations. _____

3. Choose another regular polygon and create your own tessellation in the space below. Use reflection and rotation to create your tessellation. It may be helpful to cut out the shape you choose to use it as a tracing guide.

4. Show your tesselation to a friend and see if they can identify the lines of symmetry in your tesselation.